The Rational Emotive Behavior Therapy Pocket Companion for Clients

The REBT Pocket Companion for Clients

by

Windy Dryden

ALBERT ELLIS INSTITUTE • NEW YORK, NY
www.rebt.org

FIRST EDITION

Published by the
Albert Ellis Institute
45 East 65th Street, New York, NY 10021

PRINTED IN THE UNITED STATES OF AMERICA

Library of Congress Control Number 2003105939

ISBN 0-917476-27-1

I dedicate this book to Albert Ellis for the phenomenal contribution he has made to Rational Emotive Behavior Therapy (REBT), Cognitive Behavior Therapy (CBT), and general psychotherapy. In light of this contribution and to mark Al Ellis' 90th birthday, I have donated royalties from this book to the Albert Ellis Institute.

Windy Dryden

Foreword

Windy Dryden has done it again! After writing almost innumerable authoritative books for psychotherapists and for the public on Rational Emotive Behavior Therapy, he now has produced *The REBT Pocket Companion for Clients*. This simple but still profound self-help book briefly and very clearly informs you exactly what you can — and preferably should — do to collaborate with your therapist to help bring about and maintain rational thinking, together with healthy feelings and behaviors. The book is short but (very) sweet!

It would be difficult for anyone (including me) to discover anything significant that this Pocket Companion has omitted. If you are engaged in REBT therapy, it describes important issues that will often arise — including goal setting; the assessing and disputing of irrational beliefs; dealing with the main kinds of disturbances that your irrational beliefs accompany; unconditional acceptance of yourself, other people, and world conditions; cognitive, emotional, and behavioral homework; how to confront your therapist when you disagree with her; how to recognize and dispute your meta-emotional problems (that is, your emotional problems about your having emotional problems); how you can forcefully substitute rational beliefs for your irrational ones; and almost anything else that you may have trouble with during your REBT therapy or when you use REBT on your own. Maybe Windy has omitted some important aspects of your being in Rational Emotive Behavior Therapy or Cognitive Behavior Therapy, but I doubt it!!

All told, the most relevant beginning, middle, and end of your REBT therapy are remarkably well covered in this Pocket Companion. As Windy concludes, "Use this book without becoming dependent on its use." Yes, as REBT urges, with its help you can think, feel, and act a hell of a lot better!

Albert Ellis, Ph.D., President
Albert Ellis Institute
45 East 65th Street
New York, NY 10021
email: aiellis@aol.com

Introduction

I have compiled the material in this book and have presented it in this format of one self-help tip per page to help you get the most out of Rational Emotive Behavior Therapy (REBT). Each of the tips is fairly short to help you take a moment during your busy day to think about your therapy and how you can best apply REBT. All 240 of these tips serve as reminders about basic aspects of REBT theory and practice, to help you to assess your problems and find the best way of tackling these problems right then and there.

I suggest that you read through the *REBT Pocket Companion for Clients* once so that you know what is in it, then turn to the particular pages containing the tips that are most relevant for you at any point in time. You can even keep certain pages "bookmarked" for future reference, to remind you of the things you need to work on. This book is meant to supplement your use of other self-help material, not to replace it. It has been designed so that you can carry it around with you in your pocket or purse and look through it when you have a free moment — or when you want concise self-help tips.

I hope that you find this book to be a valuable REBT self-help resource.

Windy Dryden
April, 2003

- [ ] REBT is a psycho-educational approach to therapy. Your therapist's job is to help you to learn how this approach to therapy sees your problems and sets about helping you to tackle them. Once your therapist has outlined what REBT is and how it can help you, if you think you can make use of it, fine. Give your informed consent to proceed. However, if you think that REBT is not for you, don't despair. Your therapist will be happy to refer you to a therapist with an approach that better fits what you are looking for.

❑ You may have heard that the most important ingredient in psychotherapy is the relationship between therapist and client. The REBT perspective on this issue is different. It is that while a good working alliance between you and your therapist is important, on its own it will not help you to overcome your emotional problems. The skill of your therapist in explaining relevant concepts and in teaching you important change-related techniques — and your ongoing commitment to implementing these techniques in your everyday life — are more important therapeutic ingredients.

❑ Having said that, unless you are able to disclose your problems fully to your therapist and feel a level of trust in her and her expertise, you may be well advised to seek another REBT therapist.

- [ ] During REBT, your therapist will mainly take an active-directive approach to helping you. This means that after learning about your problems, she will be active in directing you to important factors that determine your problems, and in helping you to learn productive ways of tackling them. REBT is therefore primarily a problem-focused and problem-solving approach to therapy.

- [ ] To get the most out of REBT at the beginning, make a list of the problems you want help with, and write down what you want to achieve as a result of tackling these problems during therapy. Show this to your therapist, who will help you to get the most from this list of problems and goals.

Problems

1. Sex Addiction
2. Intimacy
3. Futuretripping
4. Motivation/willingness
5.

- ❑ You will get the most from REBT if you set specific goals that are within your power to achieve. Sadly, REBT cannot help you to change others or to change external situations, since these are beyond your direct control. However, REBT can help you to change your behavior so that you increase your chances of influencing others to change, and of bringing about change in external situations.

- ❑ REBT distinguishes between practical and emotional problems. If you want to solve your practical problems during therapy, the best way that REBT can aid you is by helping you to deal first with any emotional problems you have about these practical problems.

- ❑ If you are seeking REBT for your emotional problems, it is likely that you experience one or more of the following unhealthy negative emotions: anxiety, depression, guilt, shame, hurt, unhealthy anger, unhealthy jealousy and unhealthy envy. Consult this list if you need help in identifying your disturbed emotions.

❑ During REBT, your therapist is very likely to use the ABC framework to help you assess your emotional problems accurately. "A" stands for the adversity that you are disturbed about; "B" stands for your beliefs about this "A." As you will presently see, these beliefs can either be rational and self-helping or irrational and self-impairing. "C" stands for the emotional, behavioral and thinking consequences of these beliefs.

- You may confuse your feelings at C with adversities at A. Thus, you may say that you feel rejected or feel insulted. In reality, you have been rejected or insulted (or think that you have been) at A; and you have feelings about these adversities at C. If you use the eight-emotion framework presented in the previous point, then you will be able to help yourself to be clearer about what are your feelings at C and what are adversities at A.

❑ Irrational beliefs at B in the ABC framework have the following characteristics:

a) They are rigid and extreme.
b) They are inconsistent with reality.
c) They are illogical or nonsensical.
d) They largely lead to dysfunctional emotive, behavioral, and thinking consequences.
e) They largely impede you as you pursue your healthy goals.
f) They largely interfere with your productive work and interpersonal relationships.

- ❑ Epictetus, the famous Roman philosopher, said that men are disturbed not by things, but by their views of things. The REBT version of this is as follows: “People are disturbed not by things, but by their rigid and extreme views of things.”

❑ REBT outlines four major irrational beliefs:

a) Rigid demands (*e.g.*, musts, oughts, absolute shoulds, got to's)

b) Awfulizing beliefs (*e.g.*, "It's terrible that . . . "; "It's awful that . . . "; "It's the end of the world that . . . ")

c) Low frustration tolerance (LFT) beliefs (*e.g.*, "I can't bear it"; "It's intolerable.")

d) Depreciation beliefs (*e.g.*, "I'm no good"; "You're no good"; "Life is no good.")

- [ ] In understanding your emotional problems, you may find the concept of the personal domain useful. Your personal domain includes anything and anyone that is important to you.

❑ If you suffer from anxiety, you may find the following helpful in assessing your anxiety problem:

A = You experience a *threat* to your personal domain (e.g., to your self-esteem or to your sense of comfort).

B = Irrational beliefs

C			
C	(emotional)	=	Anxiety
	(behavioral)	=	Engaging in safety-seeking behavior: avoiding threat; withdrawing from threat.
	(thinking)	=	Creating an even greater threat in your mind; underestimating your ability to deal with the threat.

- [ ] If you suffer from depression, you may find the following helpful in assessing your depression problem:

A = You have suffered a *loss* from or *failure* within your personal domain (*e.g.,* with respect to your sense of autonomy or to your connection to others).

B = Irrational beliefs

C (emotional) = Depression

(behavioral) = Withdrawing from reinforcements into self; sleeping excessively; being inactive.

(thinking) = Focusing on the negative; thinking that the future is hopeless; thinking that you are helpless.

- ❑ If you suffer from guilt, you may find the following helpful in assessing your guilt problem:

A = *Transgressing a moral rule* in your personal domain (*i.e.,* doing the wrong thing);
Failing to abide by a moral rule in your personal domain (*i.e.,* not doing the right thing);
Harming and/or hurting the feelings of someone significant in your personal domain.

B = Irrational beliefs

C		
(emotional)	=	Guilt
(behavioral)	=	Begging for forgiveness; engaging in self-punishing behavior.
(thinking)	=	Assuming far more responsibility than is warranted; giving others far less responsibility than is warranted; not taking into account mitigating factors.

- [ ] If you suffer from shame, you may find the following helpful in assessing your shame problem:

A = *You have fallen very short* of your ideal within your personal domain before a real or imagined audience.

B = Irrational beliefs

C (emotional) = Shame

(behavioral) = Removing yourself from the gaze of others; isolating yourself from others.

(thinking) = Overestimating the amount and degree of negative judgment received from others.

- [ ] If you suffer from hurt, you may find the following helpful in assessing your hurt problem:

A = Significant others in your personal domain have *let you down* and you think that you are *undeserving* of such treatment.

B = Irrational beliefs

C (emotional)	=	Hurt
(behavioral)	=	Shutting down the channel of open communication between yourself and the other(s); sulking.
(thinking)	=	Thinking that the other person does not care about you; thinking of yourself as alone, uncared for, and misunderstood.

- [ ] If you suffer from unhealthy anger, you may find the following helpful in assessing your unhealthy anger problem:

  A = Another has threatened your self-esteem; another has transgressed an important rule within your personal domain; another has frustrated your attempts to achieve an important goal within your personal domain.

  B = Irrational beliefs

  C (emotional) = Unhealthy anger

  (behavioral) = Attacking the other in some way; withdrawing aggressively.

  (thinking) = Thinking about gaining revenge; not being able to see the other's point of view.

❑ If you suffer from unhealthy jealousy, you may find the following helpful in assessing your unhealthy jealousy problem:

A = You perceive that another poses a threat to a valued relationship within your personal domain.

B = Irrational beliefs

C (emotional)	=	Unhealthy jealousy
(behavioral)	=	Seeking constant reassurance from the person with whom you have the relationship that the threat does not exist, but doubting their responses; checking the movements of your significant other; restricting the movements of your significant other.
(thinking)	=	Constructing images of your significant other's having a relationship with the other person; thinking that the loss of your relationship is imminent.

- ❑ If you suffer from unhealthy envy, you may find the following helpful in assessing your unhealthy envy problem:

  A = Another person possesses and/or enjoys something (or someone) deemed valuable within your personal domain which you do not have.

  B = Irrational beliefs

  C (emotional) = Unhealthy envy

  (behavioral) = Seeking what the other person has even when it is self-defeating to do so; disparaging or trying to destroy what the other person has.

  (thinking) = Thinking about how to get what the other person has (when it is self-defeating to do so) or how to spoil that person's enjoyment of it.

❑ It is best to deal with your emotional problems one at a time. Work on one problem until you can cope reasonably with it. In REBT this is known as your "target problem." Then switch to another problem. Don't switch from problem to problem unless you are preoccupied with a new problem and are not able to focus upon the one you have been working on.

- [ ] When working on a target problem, it is useful to select a specific example of this problem to work through. Doing so will help you and your therapist to assess the problem accurately, using the ABC framework. Stay with this specific example for the purposes of assessment, and don't switch to discussing other relevant situations.

- ❑ One of the main purposes of assessing your problems using the ABC framework is to help you to see that your unhealthy negative emotions, behavior, and distorted thinking at C are largely determined by your irrational beliefs at B, and not by the adversities that you encounter at A. If you do not understand this or don't agree with it, please make this clear to your therapist, who will spend time discussing it with you.

- [ ] You may think that REBT is saying that psychological problems are caused by irrational beliefs and that this is overly simplistic. You would be wrong if you thought this. REBT does not say that psychological problems are caused by irrational beliefs. It actually says that emotions, behavior, and thinking (including beliefs) interact in complex ways, but that irrational beliefs lie at the core of this interaction and largely account for the presence of psychological problems. Thus, in REBT, while your therapist will focus on your irrational beliefs, she will also consider your feelings, your behavior, and other forms of your thinking.

- [ ] You may think that severe adversities, such as being raped or having a loved one murdered, cause psychological disturbance. While this is understandable, it is again wide of the mark. Such atrocities do cause great distress, but distress is based on rational thinking. Disturbance is different from distress in that it is based on irrational thinking. So the goal of REBT in these cases is to help you to work through your great distress about severe adversities, while freeing yourself from the interfering presence of disturbance.

- [ ] When outlining a specific example of your target problem, you may see that you have distorted what happened at A. Since the purpose of assessment is helping you to understand how you disturbed yourself in this situation, it is important that you assume temporarily that your perception of A was correct and that you don't challenge your distortion at A yet. This will help you to identify your irrational belief at B, which was the major determinant of your disturbance. Your therapist will frequently urge you to assume temporarily that A is correct, for the same reason.

- [ ] The best time to challenge your distorted interpretations of A is when you get yourself to think rationally at B. Otherwise, your challenge will be colored and biased by your irrational beliefs at B.

- [ ] Becoming rational does not mean that you will be cold and unemotional. You can be rational (*i.e.*, flexible and non-extreme) and passionate at the same time.

- ❑ Your therapist is not going to tell you what to feel, what to do or what to think at C. Rather, she will help you to understand that you have three options about what to believe at B about adversities at A: (i) rational beliefs; (ii) irrational beliefs; or (iii) false indifference beliefs — in which you try to convince yourself that things don't matter to you when they really do. Your therapist will help you to see what are the likely emotional, behavioral and thinking consequences of each of these belief options. Then, once you have understood this, your therapist's job is to help you choose the belief option that best helps you to achieve your healthy emotional, behavioral and thinking goals.

- [ ] You may frequently hear your REBT therapist mention the word “acceptance.” In REBT, this term means the following:

    a) An acknowledgment that an adversity exists;

    b) A realization that unfortunately all the conditions are in place for the adversity to exist;

    c) An evaluation that the adversity is bad, but not awful, and that you can tolerate it; and

    d) A determination to change the adversity if it can be changed, and to deal with it as constructively as possible if it can’t be changed.

As such, acceptance differs from demanding non-acceptance (a dogmatic insistence that the adversity must not exist) and from resignation (an acknowledgment that the adversity exists, but believing that nothing can be done about it, since it cannot be changed). If you find yourself resisting the REBT concept of acceptance, list your objections to the concept and discuss these with your therapist.

❑ Realize that when you accept someone for acting badly, you are not condoning that person's behavior. You are disliking or hating the sin, but accepting the person who committed it.

- [ ] Recognize that when you accept yourself for acting badly, you are not letting yourself off the hook or excusing your actions. Rather, you are accepting full responsibility for your behavior, but without depreciating yourself for doing what you did.

❑ Acceptance also does not encourage complacency, as some people think. When you are complacent you think that you and things are O.K. and that there is no need to change anything. While acceptance is based upon an acknowledgment of reality about yourself and about what is going on, it does not preclude your trying to change negative aspects of yourself or of life, if these can be changed.

- [ ] If you are sensitive and value your sensitivity, be aware that your REBT therapist will do nothing to encourage you to be insensitive or even less sensitive. However, if you are oversensitive, meaning that your sensitivity is colored by disturbance, then you will be invited to remain sensitive, but to give up your disturbance.

- ❑ If you do not teach others where your boundaries lie, then these people are likely to cross them. If you are stopping yourself from setting boundaries with others, look for the implicit demands you are making about yourself and others that lie at the core of your failure to assert your healthy boundaries. For example, demanding that others must always approve of you will stop you from healthily asserting yourself. If you find such demands, challenge and change them — and act on your non-dogmatic preferences by asserting yourself.

- [ ] You are likely to get obnoxious behavior from others when you put up with this behavior and don't actively protest against it. Identify and deal with your obstacles to making such protests, and then make them.

- [ ] When you demand that you mustn't have problems, doing so doesn't get rid of these problems; it multiplies them.

- [ ] Don't accept something as true because an authority has said it, even if that authority is your therapist. Use your brain, not hers.

- [ ] You may think that the only alternative to selfishness is selflessness. If so, you'd be wrong. Enlightened self-interest or self-care is another option and is, in fact, the healthiest of the three positions — since it involves your looking after yourself while being actively mindful of the interests of others.

- [ ] Consider applying the "baseball rule" to life. When you do something (correctly) three times and it doesn't work, it is time to "strike out" and use a different approach.

- [ ] Have you gone to therapy with the goal of becoming "normal?" If so, you may be selling yourself short, since you could rather strive to be *healthy.* For "healthy" is based on rational thinking, while "normal" often isn't. Discuss this difference with your REBT therapist if you are unclear about it.

- [ ] Nobody presses your buttons. If you had buttons, you would be the one pressing them.

- [ ] Some people think wrongly that REBT therapists discourage their clients from discussing their pasts. So if you want to discuss past events with your therapist, do so, but understand that the only productive things you can do about the past are to undisturb yourself about it and then to learn from it.

- ❑ Your therapist may well at times encourage you to stand back and reflect on the work that you are doing together. Feel free to initiate this reflection with your therapist, particularly if you have concerns about how therapy is proceeding.

- ❑ While REBT can often be a short-term therapy, if you have significant and/or entrenched psychological problems, you may well need much longer-term therapy to effectively address these problems.

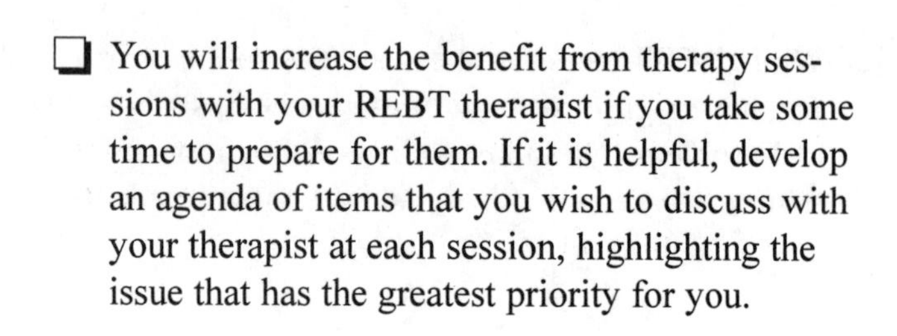

❑ You will increase the benefit from therapy sessions with your REBT therapist if you take some time to prepare for them. If it is helpful, develop an agenda of items that you wish to discuss with your therapist at each session, highlighting the issue that has the greatest priority for you.

- [ ] Your therapist may well ask you periodically to summarize your understanding of what she has been saying. Her purpose is not to test you, but to ensure that she has made herself clear in her communications with you.

- [ ] Tell your therapist what you find helpful and unhelpful about REBT. This will enable her to help you to capitalize on the former and to minimize the latter.

- ❑ While your REBT therapist is likely to take an active-directive stance, particularly at the beginning of therapy, as you improve over time she will encourage you to do more of the therapeutic work for yourself both inside and outside therapy.

- [ ] Both you and your therapist have different roles to play in therapy. Your role as a client is to:

    - Disclose and specify your problems.
    - Be open to the REBT framework.
    - Apply the principle of emotional responsibility (that you disturb yourself about adversities).
    - Put into practice outside therapy sessions what you learn within them.
    - Disclose your doubts, reservations and objections about REBT.
    - Be open about your contribution to obstacles to therapeutic change.

Ask your therapist to tell you how she sees her role as an REBT therapist. Discuss with your therapist any matters arising from this specification of your respective roles.

- [ ] You may find it helpful to make notes in therapy sessions, to facilitate later recall of what you discussed in therapy and what salient points your therapist made.

- [ ] You may also find it helpful to tape-record your therapy sessions and review the tapes later to increase what you learn from these sessions, since you may have missed some important points in the heat of the therapeutic discussion.

- ❑ Take time to think about your answers to your therapist's questions. Well thought-through answers are frequently more useful then quick, off-the-cuff responses. So, if your therapist is not giving you ample time to think about your answers to her questions, slow her down.

- [ ] It is a feature of ordinary conversation that people may ramble, go off the point, or change the topic. Therapeutic conversation in REBT is different. It is orderly, structured and focused on your problems and their remediation. So, if you ramble, go off the point, or change the topic, your therapist will tactfully interrupt you and bring you back to the agreed-upon therapeutic focus.

- [ ] Actively work on your problems with your therapist from the very beginning of therapy. You don't need to give her the "big picture" of your life before starting to work on your problems. She will build up an overall picture of you and your problems over time.

- ❑ If you have practical problems that you want to discuss with your therapist, realize that you are best equipped to deal with these practical problems once you have dealt with your disturbed emotions about these practical problems.

- ☐ Be alert to the fact that you may have emotional problems about your emotional problems (these are called "secondary" or "meta-emotional" problems in REBT). However, do not assume that these are always present.

- [ ] If you have a secondary or meta-emotional problem about your target problem, work on this first, if:
   (i) its presence interferes with the work you are doing with your therapist on your target problem within therapy sessions;
   (ii) its presence interferes with your between-session work on your target problem;
   (iii) it is clinically more important than the target problem (your therapist will help you on this point);
   (iv) you can see the sense of working on your secondary or meta-emotional problem first.

- [ ] In therapy, you may discover that you have a tendency to disturb yourself. If so, it is important that you accept yourself for having this tendency. If you blame yourself for this, then: *(a)* you will, in the first place, disturb yourself for having this tendency, something that is outside your control; and *(b)* you will, in the second place, stop yourself from working steadily to counteract this tendency.

- [ ] If you do not understand the REBT terminology used by your therapist, ask her to explain what these terms mean. Then make sure that your understanding is accurate.

- [ ] You don't have to use REBT terminology in therapy. Rather, use your own words to reflect REBT concepts.

- [ ] Try to use B-C language (*e.g.*, "I made myself disturbed about my boss's criticism") rather than A-C language (*e.g.*, "My boss's criticism disturbed me.") Doing so will help you to take blame-free responsibility for your disturbed feelings, and also help you to focus on and change the irrational beliefs with which you disturbed yourself.

- [ ] If your attempts to use B-C language in therapy are too inhibiting, discuss this with your therapist. She will in all probability encourage you to express yourself in your own uninhibited way.

- [ ] If you don't understand the purpose of your therapist's interventions, ask her to explain.

- [ ] Give your therapist feedback on the helpfulness or unhelpfulness of her interventions. Otherwise, she may continue to use interventions that you do not find useful.

❑ REBT's ABC model of psychological disturbance stresses the central role that irrational beliefs play in determining psychological disturbance. In doing this, REBT does not imply that adversities at A play an unimportant role in your problems. Such adversities contribute significantly to your disturbance, even though they do not determine it.

- [ ] If you are adamant that very adverse events have caused your emotional problems, it is important that you distinguish between the origin and maintenance of emotional problems. Even if you are correct in stating that the adversities in question originally caused your emotional problems, you are still actively keeping this disturbance alive in the present by the irrational beliefs that you hold now about events that happened then. Please note that you can do something now to change these presently-held irrational beliefs.

- [ ] If you need inspiration to overcome great tragedy, you might find this quote from Viktor Frankl useful:

  "We who lived in concentration camps can remember the men who walked through the huts comforting others, giving away their last piece of bread. They may have been small in number, but they offer sufficient proof that everything can be taken away from a man but one thing: the last of human freedoms — to choose one's attitude in any given set of circumstances, to choose one's way."

- [ ] Once your therapist has taught you the principle of emotional responsibility (that you largely disturb yourself), remind yourself of this frequently, because it is easy to lapse back into the idea that events disturb you (or what might be called the "principle of emotional irresponsibility").

- ❑ If while trying to implement REBT's principle of emotional responsibility, you find yourself blaming yourself for disturbing yourself, discuss this with your therapist. She will help you to see that you are responsible, but are not damnable for being responsible.

- [ ] Contrary to what some critics may think, REBT does not neglect your emotions. Far from it. In fact, REBT places your emotions center stage in therapy.

- [ ] In REBT, it is sufficient for you to identify your disturbed feelings and then use this information to identify, challenge and change the irrational beliefs that underpin them. You do not have to discuss every nook and cranny of your feelings in REBT, unless doing so has some real therapeutic benefit for you. If in doubt, discuss this issue with your therapist.

- [ ] An important goal of REBT is to help you to experience healthy negative emotions in the face of life's adversities. While it is not healthy to disturb yourself about such adversities, it is also not healthy for you to feel calm or indifferent when they occur.

- [ ] Most of the time you have problems because you experience unhealthy negative emotions about life's adversities, but some of the time you may have problems because you do not experience healthy negative emotions about these adversities. In the latter case, your therapist will help you to identify, challenge and change the irrational beliefs with which you prevent yourself from feeling healthily negative.

❑ What constitutes a set of healthy alternatives to unhealthy negative emotions? The following is one approach to this:

Unhealthy Negative Emotion	Healthy Negative Emotion
Anxiety	Concern
Depression	Sadness
Guilt	Remorse
Shame	Disappointment
Hurt	Sorrow
Unhealthy anger	Healthy anger
Unhealthy jealousy	Healthy jealousy
Unhealthy envy	Healthy envy

- [ ] Although REBT uses specific words to distinguish healthy from unhealthy negative emotions (*e.g.*, concern vs. anxiety and remorse vs. guilt), you do not have to use these terms. Rather, use an emotional language that is meaningful to you, and make sure that your therapist understands your personalized emotional language.

- ❑ Consider your reactions to what REBT considers to be unhealthy negative emotions (whatever specific terms you decide to use when referring to them). Just because these emotions are deemed unhealthy by REBT theory, it does not automatically follow that you will wish unequivocally to target them for change. Discuss this issue with your therapist, if relevant.

- [ ] Your REBT therapist will not only assess your unhealthy negative emotions at C in the ABC framework; she will also assess your dysfunctional behavior and distorted thinking at C. So, get used to identifying all three C's — unhealthy negative emotions, dysfunctional behavior, and distorted thinking — in your everyday life.

- [ ] When describing the adversities at A about which you have disturbed yourself, be succinct. Your therapist does not need an enormous amount of information about what happened at A in order to help you to identify your disturbed reactions at C and your underlying irrational beliefs at B.

- ☐ When you describe specific examples of target problems, your therapist will probably help you to identify the aspect of the troublesome situation that you were most disturbed about. This is called the "critical A" in REBT. You can gain practice in identifying your critical A's by asking this question: "In this situation, what did I make myself most disturbed about?" If you know your disturbed emotional C, you can use this in your question, *e.g.,* "In this situation, what did I make myself most anxious about?"

❑ You may wonder whether to treat frustration as an A or as a C. In my view it is most useful to treat it as an A — a block to the realization of your goals. But if you want to treat it as a C, distinguish between feelings of healthy frustration (prompting creative problem-solving to overcome the block) and feelings of unhealthy frustration (prompting impulsive, self-defeating action).

- [ ] When formulating an ABC assessment, it may become clear that you have distorted the situation at A. However, unless there is good reason to do otherwise, refrain from challenging distorted inferences at A until you have identified and disputed irrational beliefs at B, since these irrational beliefs are the prime determinants of your emotional problem. This point holds true when you are outlining the specific example of your target problem (see p. 28) or when you are assessing it (as here).

❑ When working with irrational beliefs, the following rules of thumb are useful:

a) identify and dispute your demand and your self-depreciation belief, if your problem is related to lowered self-esteem.

b) identify and dispute your demand and your other-depreciation belief, if you have an unhealthy other-directed anger problem.

c) identify and dispute your demand and awfulizing or LFT belief for all other problems.

- [ ] It is important to distinguish clearly between *absolute* shoulds and other shoulds (*e.g.*, conditional shoulds, recommendatory shoulds, ideal shoulds, empirical shoulds, and shoulds of preference). Target only your absolute shoulds for change in REBT, since these are the only shoulds that underpin your disturbed feelings. A typical absolute should is, "I absolutely should do well at all times at work, no matter what happens." A typical conditional should is, "If I want to pass my examination I should work hard."

- [ ] Answer the following two questions:

  (a) Do you want to improve very quickly, at a moderate speed, or slowly?

  (b) Do you want to exert much effort, moderate effort, or little effort while helping yourself to change?

If you want to improve very quickly while expending little effort, you are looking for magic. In general, the speed of your improvement is proportional to the amount of effort you are prepared to devote to self-help.

- [ ] Strive to achieve a balance between your short-term goals and your longer-term goals. If you overly focus on your long-term goals, your life may well be devoid of fun; and if you overly focus on your short-term goals, you may experience little meaning and purpose and mainly bring about unlasting satisfaction.

- ❑ If you set therapeutic goals that unwittingly perpetuate your irrational beliefs and dysfunctional feelings and behaviors, your REBT therapist will discuss this with you and help you to set more healthy goals.

- [ ] It is important that you set therapeutic goals that are within your power to achieve.

- [ ] State your therapeutic goals in positive terms (*e.g.,* "I want to feel concerned about...") and not in negative terms (*e.g.,* "I don't want to feel anxious about..."). It is often far easier to work towards the presence of something than towards the absence of something.

- [ ] Work towards therapeutic goals that are based on overcoming disturbance before you work towards goals that are based on furthering your personal development. Otherwise your disturbed feelings may block your personal development work.

- [ ] Set therapeutic goals that are neither overwhelmingly high nor underwhelmingly low. Tackle the irrational beliefs that underpin such unrealistic goal-setting.

- [ ] Once you have set your therapeutic goals, make a commitment to achieving them, and keep renewing this commitment.

- [ ] If you are ambivalent about making a commitment to achieving your therapeutic goals, carry out a cost-benefit analysis to better understand your reservations about change. Deal with these reservations constructively, and then make a commitment to goal achievement. If you are still unable to make one, identify and target for change the irrational beliefs that you have about making such a commitment.

- The major goal of REBT is not only to promote rational thinking, but also to promote healthy living based on rational thinking.

- ❑ Review your therapeutic goals as therapy proceeds. Don't assume that the goals you set at the beginning of REBT therapy will still be relevant in the middle or later phases of therapy.

- ❑ Once your REBT therapist has helped you to identify your irrational beliefs at B, and you understand that these irrational beliefs are the major reasons for your disturbed reactions at C, she will help you to stand back and question these irrational beliefs. This is known as “disputing irrational beliefs.”

- [ ] While disputing your irrational beliefs, your therapist will help you to:
    - See why your irrational beliefs are irrational.
    - Formulate rational alternatives to these irrational beliefs.
    - See why your rational beliefs are rational.

❑ **Irrational beliefs** are false, illogical, and generally yielding of poor results. Your therapist will help you to understand these points by asking you questions such as:

Irrational beliefs are false: "Is it true that you *must*...?"; "What evidence is there that you cannot tolerate...?"; "Just because you acted badly, is that support for the idea that you are a bad person?"

Irrational beliefs are illogical: "Is it logical to conclude that just because you *want to* [do something], that therefore you *must* do it?"; "Does it logically follow that because you acted badly, the whole of you is bad through and through?"

Irrational beliefs generally yield poor results: "What are the consequences of believing that you *must* ... ?"; "Will thinking that you are a bad person for acting badly help you to reach your goals?"

❑ **Demands** (musts, absolute shoulds, got to's) are irrational for the following reasons:

They are false: If there were a law of the universe that stated that you absolutely must do well, then you could not fail to do well. It would be impossible for you to fail. This is obviously untrue.

They are illogical: A demand is made up of two components — a non-rigid component (*e.g.,* "I want to do well") and a rigid component ("... therefore I must do well"). The latter does not logically follow from the former, since you logically cannot derive something rigid from something that is non-rigid.

They generally yield poor results: While demands may have some positive results (*e.g.,* they may be motivating), by and large most of the results they yield are poor (*e.g.,* they result in anxiety; thus their motivating effect is contaminated with anxiety and with the inefficiency that often goes with it).

- [ ] **Awfulizing beliefs** ("It's terrible that..."; "It's awful that..."; "It's the end of the world that...") are irrational for the following reasons:

  They are false: Awful means that nothing could be worse and that no good could possibly come from bad. This is untrue since things can virtually always be worse than they are and good can come from bad. Awful also means that something is so bad that it absolutely must not exist. But no matter how bad it is, it unfortunately does exist.

  They are illogical: An awfulizing belief is made up of two components — a non-extreme component (*e.g.*, "It is bad if I do not do well") and an extreme component ("...therefore it is awful"). The latter does not logically follow from the former, since you logically cannot derive something extreme from something that is non-extreme.

  They generally yield poor results: Same argument as with "demands," as stated previously.

❑ **Low frustration tolerance (LFT)** beliefs ("I can't bear it"; "It's intolerable") are irrational for the following reasons:

They are false: LFT beliefs mean that you will either die, disintegrate or lose the capacity for happiness if what you deem to be intolerable exists. None of these is likely to happen.

They are illogical: An LFT belief has two components – a non-extreme component (*e.g.,* "It's difficult to tolerate…") and an extreme component ("…therefore it is intolerable"). The latter does not logically follow from the former, since you logically cannot derive something extreme from something that is non-extreme.

They generally yield poor results: Same argument as with "demands" and "awfulizing beliefs," as stated previously.

- ☐ **Depreciation beliefs** (“I am bad”; “You are bad”; “Life is bad”) are irrational for the following reasons:

  They are false: Depreciation beliefs imply that you can legitimately assign a single global rating to a complex being or to the world. You cannot truthfully do this, since you, for example, are too complex to merit such a rating and you are constantly changing.

  They are illogical: A depreciation belief has two components — a rating of a part (*e.g.*, “I acted badly”) and a rating of the whole (*e.g.*, “I am bad.”) A part cannot define the whole, and thus depreciation beliefs are illogical, since they make the part-whole error.

  They generally yield poor results: Same argument as with “demands,” “awfulizing beliefs” and “LFT beliefs,” as stated previously.

- ❑ If you have difficulty answering disputing questions, your therapist will explain to you in a didactic manner why your irrational beliefs are false, illogical, and generally yielding of poor results. After doing so, she will probably ask you to put your understanding of what she said into your own words. She will be doing this not to "test" you, but rather to see whether or not her explanations are clear.

- [ ] It is important that you actively engage in the disputing process. Give honest answers and don't say what you think your therapist wants to hear or what you think are the "right" answers to her questions, when you are unsure why these "right" answers are, in fact, correct. The goal of disputing is not to help you to unthinkingly parrot rational arguments, but for you to genuinely understand and agree with the arguments that explain why your irrational beliefs are irrational and why your rational beliefs are rational. Thus, if you don't understand an argument, or if you disagree with an argument, tell your therapist about it and discuss it fully with her.

- ❑ Albert Ellis, the founder of REBT, has argued that absolutistic demands are at the very core of psychological problems and that awfulizing, LFT and depreciation beliefs are derived from these demands. However, it is often useful to dispute both your demands and their relevant irrational belief derivatives. In doing so, you may find disputing basic demands to be more meaningful than disputing their derivatives; or you may find the opposite. Concentrate on disputes that are particularly meaningful to you.

- [ ] During disputing, you need to question your rational beliefs in the same way that you questioned your irrational beliefs.

- Rational beliefs at B in the ABC framework have the following characteristics:

  (a) They are flexible and non-extreme.

  (b) They are consistent with reality.

  (c) They are logical and make sense.

  (d) They largely lead to functional emotive, behavioral and thinking consequences.

  (e) They largely help you as you pursue your healthy goals.

  (f) They largely sustain and improve your productive work and interpersonal relationships.

❑ REBT outlines four major **rational beliefs:**

(a) **Non-dogmatic preferences** (in which you acknowledge what you want, but you actively assert that you do not have to get what you want).

(b) **Anti-awfulizing beliefs** (in which you acknowledge that it is bad when you don't get what you want, but you actively assert that it isn't the end of the world).

(c) **High frustration tolerance beliefs (HFT)** (in which you acknowledge that it is a struggle putting up with not getting your desires met. However, you actively assert that you can tolerate this, and recognize that it is well worth tolerating).

(d) **Acceptance beliefs** (in which you acknowledge that both you and others are complex, unratable, unique, fallible human beings who are constantly in flux. You also acknowledge that life is incredibly rich and complex, and can definitely not be given a single fixed, global rating).

❑ **Rational beliefs** are true, logical, and generally yield good results. Your therapist will help you to understand these points by asking you questions such as:

- ***Rational beliefs are true:*** "Is it true that you want, but don't have to...?"; "What evidence is there that you can tolerate...even though it is difficult for you to do so?"; "Can you support the idea that you are a fallible human being who can act in good and bad ways rather than a bad person for acting badly?"
- ***Rational beliefs are logical:*** "Is it sensible for you to conclude that you don't have to get something even though you want it?"; "Does it logically follow that because you acted badly, therefore you are a fallible human being who can act in good and bad ways?"
- ***Rational beliefs generally yield good results:*** "What are the consequences of believing that you want to do...but don't have to do it?"; "Will thinking that you are not a bad person for acting badly, but a fallible human being, help you to reach your goals?"

❑ **Non-dogmatic preferences** ("I want to, but I don't have to") are rational for the following reasons:

- ***They are true:*** You can prove that your preferences are true, and it is also true that you do not have to have what you want.

- ***They are logical:*** A non-dogmatic preference (*e.g.,* "I want to do well, but I don't have to do well") is made up of two non-rigid components that are logically connected since both are non-rigid.

- ***They generally yield good results:*** While non-dogmatic preferences may have one or two poor results *(e.g.,* they may initially be less motivating than demands), by and large most of the results they yield are good (*e.g.,* they result in healthy rather than unhealthy negative emotions if adversities are encountered, and are more motivating in the longer run).

- ☐ **Anti-awfulizing beliefs** ("It is bad, but it isn't awful") are rational for the following reasons:

  - ***They are true:*** You can prove that it is bad when your preferences are not met; and you can also prove that it is isn't awful when this happens, because *(i)* worse things could always happen, and *(ii)* good things can come from these bad events.

  - ***They are logical:*** An anti-awfulizing belief (*e.g.,* "It is bad when I don't do well, but it isn't awful") is made up of two non-extreme components that are logically connected, since both are non-extreme.

  - ***They generally yield good results:*** Same arguments as with "non-dogmatic preferences," as stated previously.

❑ **High frustration tolerance beliefs** ("It is difficult to put up with, but I can tolerate it") are rational for the following reasons:

- ***They are true:*** You can prove that it is difficult to put up with not having your preferences met; and you can also prove that you can tolerate doing so, since when your preferences are not met *(i)* you will, in all probability, neither die nor disintegrate, and *(ii)* you will still retain the capacity for future happiness.

- ***They are logical:*** A high frustration tolerance belief (*e.g.,* "It is difficult to tolerate not doing well, but I can tolerate doing so") is made up of two non-extreme components that are logically connected, since both are non-extreme.

- ***They generally yield good results:*** Same arguments as with "non-dogmatic preferences" and "anti-awfulizing beliefs," as stated previously.

- ❑ **Acceptance beliefs** ("I am fallible"; "You are fallible"; "Life is a complex mixture of good, bad and neutral events") are rational for the following reasons:

  - ***They are true:*** In acceptance beliefs, you do not assign a single global rating to a complex being or to the world. Rather, you acknowledge as true that you, for example, are too complex to merit such a rating and are constantly changing.

  - ***They are logical:*** An acceptance belief has two components: *(i)* a rating of a part of you (*e.g.*, "I acted badly") or what has happened to you (*e.g.*, "Being rejected is bad"), and *(ii)* an acknowledgment that you or your life defies a single global rating (*e.g.*, "I am a fallible human being who can act well or badly.") The complexity of yourself or of your life means that a part of yourself or your experience can be incorporated into the whole, but does not define the whole. Thus, acceptance beliefs are logical, since they do not make the part-whole error.

  - ***They generally yield good results:*** Same argument as with "non-dogmatic preferences," "non-awfulizing beliefs" and "HFT beliefs," as stated previously.

- [ ] During disputing, openly debate with your therapist. Try not to argue defensively with her.

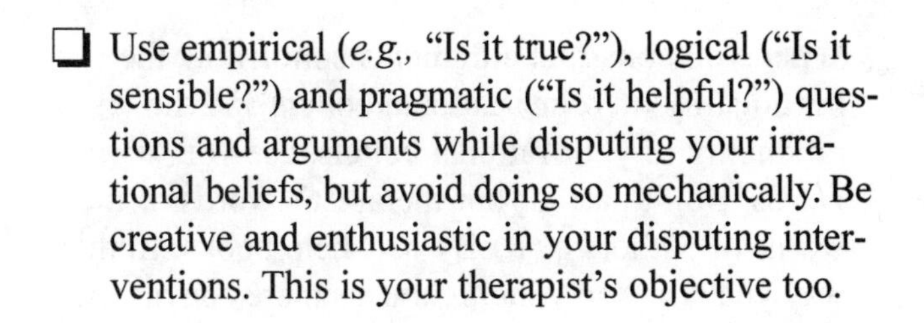

- ☐ Use empirical (*e.g.*, “Is it true?”), logical (“Is it sensible?”) and pragmatic (“Is it helpful?”) questions and arguments while disputing your irrational beliefs, but avoid doing so mechanically. Be creative and enthusiastic in your disputing interventions. This is your therapist’s objective too.

- [ ] When you construct arguments concerning the irrationality of your irrational beliefs and the rationality of your rational beliefs, use your own words. Don't parrot your therapist's words or the words of authors of REBT self-help books. In this way you will find your arguments more convincing.

- [ ] If you are confused about why certain irrational beliefs are irrational, and/or why certain rational beliefs are rational, discuss these questions with your therapist.

- ❑ Take care that you do not switch to disputing your distorted inferences at A while disputing your irrational beliefs. You can easily do this, so guard against it by reminding yourself periodically of the irrational belief you are disputing. Throughout the irrational belief disputing process, keep to the "let's assume temporarily that A is true" position.

- [ ] Remind yourself that when you hold rigid demands, you deprive yourself and others of your — and their — freedom of choice.

- [ ] Encourage yourself to put the "f" word into your thinking: *flexibility.*

- Adversities are not the end of the world; they are, unfortunately, part of the world.

- [ ] Understand and utilize the components of high frustration tolerance:
    - "It's difficult to tolerate."
    - "I can tolerate it."
    - "It's worth tolerating."
    - "I will get worse results if I do not tolerate it."

- [ ] Remind yourself of the three main principles of self-discipline:
    - “It’s worth doing.”
    - “I’m worth doing it for.”
    - “I make it harder for myself if I don’t do it.”

- [ ] Discover which arguments you find persuasive during disputing and capitalize on this discovery.

- [ ] If you disturb yourself about others, you may find doing the following helpful. First, identify the possible irrational beliefs held by these people. Then, reflect on this: these people are driven to behave badly by their irrational beliefs. This may help you to surrender your own demands that such people must not act badly.

- ❑ The more you dispute your irrational beliefs, the more you will benefit from doing so. This is known as the principle of "over-learning." Apply this principle and question both your irrational and rational beliefs regularly over time, both within and outside of therapy sessions.

- [ ] Identify which people are role models of rationality for you. Refer to them when disputing your irrational beliefs.

- ❑ It is important that you accurately distinguish between irrational and rational beliefs. In doing so, use the full version of rational beliefs, which explicitly negates irrationality.

- [ ] The full version of a preference is known as a "non-dogmatic preference." Use this full version (*e.g.*, "I very much want to pass this test, *but I really don't have to do so")* rather than the partial version which does not explicitly negate irrationality (*e.g.*, "I very much want to pass this test"). If you use the partial version you are more vulnerable to transforming it into an irrational belief (*e.g.*, "I very much want to pass this test… and therefore I have to do so").

- [ ] The full version of an anti-awfulizing belief is shown in the following example: "It is very bad if I do not pass this test, *but it isn't awful if I do not do so.*" Use this rather than the partial version which does not explicitly negate irrationality (*e.g.*, "It is very bad if I do not pass this test"). If you use the partial version you are more vulnerable to transforming it into an irrational belief (*e.g.*, "It is very bad if I do not pass this test... and therefore it is awful if I do not do so").

❑ The full version of a high frustration tolerance (HFT) belief is shown in the following example: "If I do not pass this test, it would be difficult to put up with, *but I could tolerate it.*" Use this rather than the partial version which does not explicitly negate irrationality (*e.g.,* "If I did not pass this test, it would be difficult to put up with"). If you use the partial version you are more vulnerable to transforming it into an irrational belief (*e.g.,* "If I did not pass this test, it would be difficult to put up with…and therefore it would be intolerable").

- [ ] The full version of an acceptance belief asserts who the person (in this case) is and who he is not as shown in the following example: "If I do not pass this test, that would be bad, but it would not prove that I am a failure; *it would prove that I am a fallible human capable of succeeding and failing.*" Use this rather than the partial version which only states who the person is not, since this does not explicitly negate irrationality (*e.g.,* "If I do not pass this test, that would be bad, but it would not prove that I am a failure"). If you use the partial version you are more vulnerable to transforming it into an irrational belief (*e.g.,* "If I do not pass this test that would be bad, but it would not prove that I am a failure. It would prove that I am worthier if I pass than if I fail").

- [ ] Construct rational alternatives to your irrational beliefs. In doing so, put these rational beliefs into your own words. If you are in any doubt, your therapist will check that your wording reflects rational meaning.

- ❑ If you have any doubts, reservations or objections with respect to giving up your irrational beliefs and/or committing to the rational alternatives to these beliefs, share your doubts, *etc.* with your therapist. She will engage you in an open, constructive dialogue on these issues. If you keep your doubts, *etc.* to yourself, then you hinder your progress in REBT.

❑ Once you have understood why your irrational beliefs are irrational and why your rational beliefs are rational, it is important that you make a commitment to work towards weakening your conviction in the former case and strengthening your conviction in the latter. In order to make such a commitment, you need to understand that this involves the following:

- Continuing to question your irrational and rational beliefs.
- Developing a store of arguments concerning why your irrational beliefs are irrational and why your rational beliefs are rational, and using these arguments in a forceful, energetic and persuasive fashion.
- Undertaking to act, feel, and think in ways that are consistent with your rational beliefs and inconsistent with your irrational beliefs, and doing this regularly.

- [ ] Act, feel, and think in ways that are consistent with your rational beliefs. Be alert for instances in which your behavior, feeling and thinking are inconsistent with these developing rational beliefs, and intervene accordingly.

- [ ] Using REBT with others is a good way of disputing your own irrational beliefs. However, you need to guard against imposing rational principles upon those who are not interested in them.

- [ ] Your irrational beliefs have negatively distorting effects upon your inferences at A as well as upon your subsequent thinking at C. Ask your therapist to help you to understand these effects.

- ☐ It is important to conduct behavioral experiments when you think you can't do something. But first it is helpful to challenge the irrational beliefs that lead you to think that you are incapable.

- ☐ REBT involves more than helping you to identify, challenge and change your irrational beliefs. For example, if you are deficient in relevant skills like assertiveness, your therapist will teach you these skills.

- [ ] Your therapist will teach you to use a variety of cognitive techniques to weaken your conviction in your irrational beliefs and strengthen your conviction in your rational beliefs.

- [ ] Use the rational portfolio method to develop greater conviction in your rational beliefs. This involves your keeping a written list of all the arguments you can think of in favor of your rational beliefs and against your irrational beliefs. Review this portfolio frequently.

- [ ] Write down attacks upon your rational beliefs and practice persuasively responding to these attacks. Some people call this the "attack-response technique."

- ❑ You can also practice the attack-response technique with a tape recorder. In doing so, make sure that your rational voice is more persuasive than your irrational voice, in both content and tone.

- [ ] Further develop your skills with the attack-response technique by practicing it with a friend. State your rational belief and ask your friend to persuade you to think irrationally again. Continue this dialogue until your friend has run out of irrational arguments because you have effectively responded to them.

- [ ] Finally, practice the attack-response technique with your therapist, who will increase the ferocity of her irrational attacks to match your developing skill at defending your rational beliefs.

- [ ] You often unwittingly rehearse your disturbance in the following way. During the day you may think about an adversity and, as you do so, you disturb yourself about this event by implicitly bringing your irrational beliefs to your thoughts about the adversity.

- [ ] Instead of rehearsing your disturbance, do the following. Think about the adversity in question and rehearse your rational beliefs about it until you feel healthily bad, but not unhealthily disturbed.

- [ ] There is an important difference between "feeling better" and "getting better." "Getting better" involves your dealing effectively with any present or future adversities (A's) by reacting with rational beliefs, healthy feelings and functional behaviors. So don't leave therapy when you feel better. Stay in therapy until you have largely gotten better.

- [ ] The more you tend to disturb yourself in certain areas, the harder you need to work to undisturb yourself in these areas.

- [ ] By all means identify and challenge your cognitive distortions (*e.g.*, black-and-white thinking, overgeneralization, personalizing, etc.), but recognize that you largely create these distortions when you hold irrational beliefs. Challenging your cognitive distortions is often more effective after you have challenged your underlying irrational beliefs, especially your absolutistic shoulds, oughts, and musts.

- [ ] Doing homework assignments is a very important part of REBT. Research has shown that clients who regularly do such assignments do better in REBT and CBT than those who don't.

- [ ] Some people know the theory of REBT very well, but do not apply it in their everyday lives. Don't join their ranks. Walk the rational talk, don't just talk the rational talk.

- ❑ If you are put off by the word "homework," use a different word. Don't let a word stop you from putting into practice outside of therapy what you have learned within therapy.

- ❑ Your therapist should ideally negotiate a suitable homework assignment with you at practically every therapy session. If she forgets, remind her.

- [ ] Homework assignments should ideally be based on the work that you have done with your therapist during therapy sessions. Don't wait for your therapist to suggest such assignments. Come up with ideas for homework assignments yourself.

- [ ] Read an REBT self-help book for information about how you disturb yourself and what you can do to undisturb yourself. Then put this information into practice.

- [ ] Reading self-help books is an important prelude to action, not a substitute for it.

❑ If the REBT self-help book that you are reading has exercises in it, do these exercises. Don't just passively read them.

- [ ] Keep written records of homework assignments to help you remember to do these tasks.

- ❑ There are a variety of REBT self-help forms of differing complexity. Once you have found one that is particularly helpful, use it regularly.

- [ ] Your therapist should ideally train you to use whichever self-help form you deem to be most useful. If she does not do this, ask her to do so.

- [ ] Show your therapist your completed self-help forms. When you make mistakes on these forms, your therapist will explain why these are errors and help you to correct them.

- [ ] Specify when you are going to do your homework assignments, how often, and in which situations.

- [ ] In working with you, your therapist will suggest a range of cognitive, emotive, and behavioral homework assignments (including the use of rational-emotive imagery). Before you agree to do these assignments, make sure you can see how doing them will help you achieve your therapeutic goals.

- [ ] The most powerful homework assignments are those that involve your confronting negative activating events while you are rehearsing your rational beliefs.

- [ ] Before confronting a negative activating event in reality, you might find it helpful to first do so in your imagination. As you do so, dispute your irrational belief and rehearse your rational belief.

- ❑ When confronting negative activating events, it is useful to rehearse your rational beliefs before, during and after the confrontation.

- [ ] When confronting negative activating events, it is important that you do not engage in any safety-seeking behaviors that interfere with the confrontation process. Make a list of your safety-seeking behaviors in advance, so you can guard against using them in the relevant situations.

- [ ] Negotiate with your therapist homework assignments that are challenging for you at that time, but not overwhelming.

- [ ] When carrying out behavioral homework assignments, you may very well still experience an urge to act in a well-established, but self-defeating, manner. Here it is important to distinguish between an urge to act and an overt action. Just because you feel like doing something, it doesn't mean that you have to do it. So use your urge to act in a "natural," but dysfunctional, way as a cue to act in an "unnatural," but constructive, manner.

- [ ] Carry out homework assignments for your own therapeutic benefit rather than to please your therapist. If you find yourself doing the latter, challenge and change your need for your therapist's approval.

- [ ] Troubleshoot possible obstacles to homework task completion before you do these tasks.

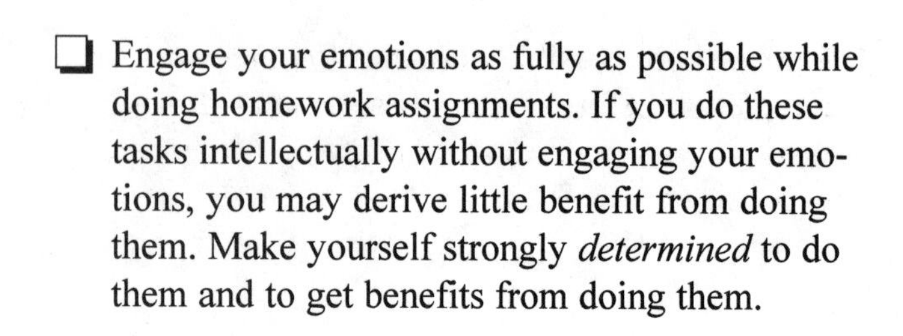

❑ Engage your emotions as fully as possible while doing homework assignments. If you do these tasks intellectually without engaging your emotions, you may derive little benefit from doing them. Make yourself strongly *determined* to do them and to get benefits from doing them.

❑ If you don't have the necessary skills to carry out a homework assignment, your therapist should ideally teach you these skills first. If not, ask her to do so.

- [ ] Commit yourself to *doing* homework assignments rather than to *trying* to do them, since trying does not necessarily mean doing.

- [ ] Review your homework assignment with your therapist at the beginning of the session that follows, unless there is a very good reason not to do so.

- [ ] If you have successfully carried out a homework assignment, ask yourself what you have learned from doing the task. Then capitalize on your learning.

❑ You may not always be able to prevent yourself from beginning to disturb yourself, but you can stop yourself from continuing to disturb yourself.

- [ ] There is an important difference between intellectual insight (a cognitive understanding of rational principles that does not lead to constructive psychological change) and emotional insight (a deep conviction of rational principles and action taken to use these principles, that does result in such change). The latter is the goal of REBT, not the former.

- [ ] You know you have intellectual insight when you say things like: "I understand it in my head, but not in my gut." In order to get "it" into your gut, you need to strongly act and think in ways that are consistent with your rational beliefs and that are inconsistent with your irrational beliefs. You need to do this regularly over time while fully engaging your emotions.

- [ ] Commit yourself to practicing daily emotional self-care even if you do not feel disturbed. In this way, the psychological work that you do is not dependent upon your disturbed feelings, but upon your decision to help yourself daily.

- [ ] Assume a self-helping role as early in the process of REBT as you are able.

- [ ] Take an active role in generalizing your learning both within a problem area (from one specific example of a target problem to others) and between problems (from one target problem to others). Don't expect to spontaneously generalize your learning (*i.e.,* without actively planning to do so).

- [ ] After you have discussed a number of problems and specific examples of your problems in therapy, your therapist will help you to look for and work on changing your core irrational beliefs (*i.e.*, irrational beliefs that are at the core of a significant number of your problems).

- [ ] During your core-belief work, your therapist will in all probability also help you to construct core rational beliefs.

- [ ] You question your core irrational beliefs (and core rational beliefs) by using methods similar to those in which you disputed your specific irrational beliefs.

❑ Your therapist will help you to understand how you perpetuate your specific and core irrational beliefs. You do this by:

- Thinking, feeling, and acting in ways that maintain these beliefs;
- Inappropriately avoiding situations in which you are likely to activate these beliefs; and
- Over-compensating for these beliefs by pretending that you do not hold them, and even thinking that you hold some opposite, rational beliefs.

- [ ] It is important to remember that "change feels strange." So keep working for change even though it feels strange.

- [ ] Your thoughts and behavior will change more quickly than your emotions. However, if you keep acting and thinking in healthy ways, your healthy feelings will eventually catch up.

- [ ] Therapeutic change is non-linear. You may take one step backward for every two that you take forward. Indeed, you may even take two steps backward and one forward. If you remind yourself of this and digest it, you won't become discouraged when you experience setbacks.

- [ ] Go over REBT principles until they become part of your general rational outlook. But don't do this mindlessly. Think deeply about these principles as you review them.

- [ ] Find fresh new ways of thinking about rational principles to stop yourself from turning off to the idea of the "same old rational stuff." If she is creative, your therapist will also do this during therapy sessions.

- [ ] Maintaining psychological well-being involves taking regular psychological exercise, in the same way that maintaining physical well-being involves taking regular physical exercise.

- [ ] When you report improvements to your therapist, she will help you to assess the bases of these changes. She will encourage you to change your irrational beliefs if you have not already done so.

- [ ] Monitor your improvement by three criteria:

  - Frequency — do you experience your problems less frequently than before?
  - Intensity — are your problems less severe/ intense than before?
  - Duration — do your problems last for shorter periods than before?

- [ ] Once you have gotten better, you still have to work to stay better.

- [ ] There are many potential obstacles to your making progress in REBT including:
  - therapist factors
  - client factors
  - therapist-client factors (including poor client-therapist matching), and
  - the negative impact of clients' significant others.

  If applicable, your therapist will assess the source of your obstacles to change and take appropriate remedial action. Work with her on this.

❑ In order to make and maintain your therapeutic gains, you need to recognize and act upon the following:

- You make yourself disturbed by the irrational beliefs you hold about events.
- You can un-disturb yourself by challenging and changing your irrational beliefs to rational beliefs.
- You need to continue this process strongly and steadily over time.

- You may hinder your progress by holding a philosophy of low frustration tolerance about the work that you need to put in to make and sustain your therapeutic gains. In this case, you need to identify, challenge and change these LFT beliefs, in thought and especially in deed.

- ❑ You may hinder your progress by believing that you must know that REBT will work before you apply it. In which case, challenge and change this demand for certainty and apply REBT without the guarantee that it will work.

- [ ] You may hinder your progress by believing that you must make REBT work and that you are a failure if you don't. Making your self-worth dependent upon your progress in REBT will either lead you to put off helping yourself, or to helping yourself anxiously. In both cases, you will hinder your progress. Use REBT techniques to help yourself after you have challenged and changed your ego-related irrational belief.

- [ ] You may well bring your irrational beliefs to therapy sessions. Try to anticipate how your iBs may affect your behavior in therapy and change these irrational beliefs, preferably before they have a detrimental impact upon your therapy. Your therapist will also be mindful of this point and will intervene accordingly.

- ☐ You can turn any healthy philosophy into an unhealthy philosophy by thinking irrationally about it. In this context, guard against thinking irrationally about your attempts to think rationally. Thus:

    - As you work towards holding non-dogmatic preferences rather than demands, don't demand that you must not make demands any more.
    - Once you spot your awfulizing beliefs, don't awfulize about your awfulizing.
    - Remind yourself that you can tolerate the presence of your low frustration tolerance beliefs.
    - Don't depreciate yourself for depreciating yourself.

❑ What you resist usually persists. So identify and deal with the factors related to your resistance.

- [ ] Whenever possible, work towards basic belief change, but realize that at times you may be unwilling or unable to do so. When this is the case, work towards inference change, behavior change, or change in troublesome aspects of your environment.

- [ ] Express your doubts, reservations and objections to your therapist concerning aspects of REBT theory and practice that you find yourself resisting. Your therapist will then deal with any misconceptions implicit in your doubts, *etc.*

- [ ] When you are reluctant to think rationally, it may be because you perceive costs of holding rational beliefs and/or perceive benefits to holding irrational beliefs. Disclose these to your therapist, who will help you to deal with these obstacles to rational thinking.

- [ ] You may be reluctant to give up your demands for a number of reasons. You may be so reluctant because you consider that your musts and demands are motivating. This may be the case in the very short term, but in the longer term, these beliefs frequently lead to impaired disturbance-related behavior. Non-dogmatic preferences, on the other hand, are both motivating and lead to action that is free from the effects of disturbance.

- [ ] You may be reluctant to give up your awfulizing beliefs for a number of reasons. You may be so reluctant because you think that if you surrender these beliefs, you are making light of the adversities that have befallen you. However, adopting anti-awfulizing beliefs does not mean that you are making light of life's tragedies. It means that you are fully acknowledging the tragedies, but are taking out the "end-of-the-world horror" connotations that you have implicitly and optionally added to them.

❑ You may be reluctant to adopt high frustration tolerance (HFT) beliefs for a number of reasons. You may be so reluctant because you think doing so means that you will put up with an adversity without doing anything to change it. However, while your holding HFT beliefs does involve your being able to tolerate adversities, it does not preclude your doing all you can to change them. In fact, HFT beliefs help you to get in to a non-disturbed, but determined frame of mind, which will help you to change the adversities if they can be changed. On the other hand, low frustration tolerance (LFT) beliefs can lead you to attempt to change adversities in an impulsive, disturbed manner.

- [ ] When you are reluctant to think rationally, realize that you will often encourage your friends and loved ones to hold the same rational beliefs that you are resisting. Why not resolve this dissonance by encouraging yourself to think in the same way that you would want your significant others to think — rationally?

- [ ] While there may be payoffs to your emotional problems, realize that these payoffs are likely to be short-term and that most of the consequences of having emotional problems are negative, particularly in the longer term. Discuss this issue with your REBT therapist.

- ❑ You may be reluctant to give up your feelings of anxiety for a number of reasons. You may be so reluctant because you have taught yourself to motivate yourself through these feelings. Anxiety will motivate you, but in a mindless, "headless-chicken" kind of way, based as it is upon irrational beliefs. Concern (the healthy alternative to anxiety), on the other hand, will motivate you, but in a healthy, clear-minded, determined way, based upon rational beliefs. You may not be used to motivating yourself through concern, but you can learn to do so. It will be worth it to you in the long term to use concern rather than anxiety as a prime motivator.

- [ ] You may be reluctant to give up your feelings of depression for a number of reasons. You may be so reluctant because you think that it is an appropriate response to a significant loss and that sadness minimizes the significance of your loss. However, depression is a disturbed response to a loss because it is based on irrational thinking and involves withdrawal from life and despair about the future. Your rejecting sadness as an appropriate response to your loss may be based on the idea that it is a mild or moderate emotion. However, it can be an intense emotion that allows you to digest your loss without withdrawing from life or despairing about the future.

- You may be reluctant to give up your feelings of guilt for a number of reasons. You may be so reluctant because you think that guilt feelings prevent you from wrongdoing. Actually, they won't. When you experience guilt, you think that you are a bad person. When you think that way about yourself, you are more likely, not less likely, to do bad things. Because that is what bad people do — bad things. Feelings of remorse, on the other hand, are based upon the idea that when you do bad things, you are responsible for your actions, but are not a bad person for doing so. Rather, you are a fallible human being, capable of acting well and badly. Feelings of remorse can help you learn why you acted badly and — since you are capable of acting well — can encourage you to use your learning to good effect in the future.

- [ ] You may be reluctant to give up your feelings of shame for a number of reasons. You may be so reluctant because you think that the threat of feeling shame will motivate you to achieve your ideal. Actually, it won't. The threat of shame will lead you to feel anxious about possibly experiencing shame and, rather than help you to concentrate upon what you are doing, will interfere with your performance — which in turn almost guarantees that you will fall short of your ideal. Disappointment (the healthy alternative to shame) is as healthily motivating as concern (see p. 216) and, while it won't guarantee that you will achieve your ideal, it will help you to come as close as you can. You may also let yourself feel ashamed of an immoral or self-harming act you did, but not feel ashamed of your entire *self* for doing it.

- [ ] You may be reluctant to give up your feelings of hurt for a number of reasons. You may be so reluctant because you think that it is normal to feel hurt when you have been let down. This may be the case, but as I pointed out on page 43, a "normal" response is not necessarily a "healthy" response. The healthy response to hurt is sorrow. Sorrow allows you to come to terms with being let down and encourages you to address this openly with the other person. Hurt, on the other hand, will lead you to withdraw from the other, often in an angry and sulky manner. If your goal is to maintain your relationships with people who let you down from time to time (and being human, all people are capable of doing that, including you), then sorrow, rather than hurt, will help you to do so.

❑ You may be reluctant to give up your feelings of unhealthy anger for a number of reasons. You may be so reluctant because you think that your response is justified by the other person's behavior. Here, it is important to distinguish between the other person's behavior and your response to it. If the other person has seriously transgressed your personal rules, this is very bad whether you feel unhealthy anger or healthy anger. The behavior stays the same, but your response is different. Healthy anger enables you to address the transgression without attacking the other person (as in unhealthy anger). It is in all probability healthier for you physically (than unhealthy anger) and you are less likely to elicit retaliation from the other person with healthy anger than with unhealthy anger. Healthy anger may be less immediately pleasurable than unhealthy anger, but is a moment of triumph with unhealthy anger worth all of the other negative consequences?

❑ You may be reluctant to give up your feelings of unhealthy jealousy for a number of reasons. You may be so reluctant because you think that it keeps you vigilant for signs of your partner's infidelity, for example. Unhealthy jealousy will keep you vigilant all right, but it will do so when there is no objective evidence of a threat to your relationship. Indeed, unhealthy jealousy and the irrational beliefs upon which it is based will lead you to interpret innocuous signs as threats to your relationship. Healthy jealousy and the rational beliefs upon which it is based will help you to be vigilant when there is a clear threat to your relationship, but it will help you to enjoy that relationship when such a threat is not present. With unhealthy jealousy, you rarely enjoy your relationship because you think that it is constantly under threat, and that this kind of threat is *terrible.*

- [ ] You may be reluctant to give up your feelings of unhealthy envy for a number of reasons. You may be so reluctant because you think that unhealthy envy motivates you to get what you covet, but don't possess. This is partially true, but the obsessive nature of unhealthy envy means that you will pursue what you covet even when doing so is self-destructive. Even if you were to get what you covet, the irrational beliefs that underpin unhealthy envy will lead you to soon drop this and focus upon something else that you covet, but don't possess. Literally, you are rarely satisfied when your envy is unhealthy. When your envy is healthy, you will sensibly pursue something that you genuinely want because you want it, not because someone else has it and you don't. When you get what you covet and your envy is healthy, then you are able to enjoy possessing it, and don't focus upon the next coveted object that is in someone else's possession and not yours.

- [ ] Your progress may be hampered because your therapist may not understand your problems clearly enough, or even at all. She may thus make suggestions based upon her partial understanding or full misunderstanding of your problems. If so, discuss this with her as a matter of urgency.

- ❑ Your progress may be hampered because your therapist may not confront you sufficiently or push you hard enough to change. If you think this is the case, discuss this with your therapist and encourage her to be tougher with you.

- ❑ Your progress may be hampered because your therapist may confront you aggressively or push you too hard to change. If you think this is the case, discuss this with your therapist and suggest that she encourage you to change without placing unhealthy demands upon you.

- [ ] Your progress may be hampered because your REBT therapist does not use REBT with you, preferring, for example, to chat with you or to practice a different type of therapy when you are precisely seeking REBT. If this is the case, confront your therapist and encourage her to use REBT with you.

- ❑ Your progress may be hampered because you and your therapist are working towards different goals. If this is happening from your point of view, bring it to the attention of your therapist and work it through with her.

- ❑ Your progress may be hampered because you may not understand how doing what your therapist suggests that you do in and/or between sessions will help you to achieve your therapeutic goals. Consequently, you may not do what she suggests or may do so half-heartedly. If this is the case, discuss it with your therapist.

- ❑ If the above six obstacles persist after you have tried to resolve them with your therapist on a number of different occasions, then it may be in your interest to seek help from a different REBT therapist.

- [ ] Learn the difference between a lapse and a relapse. A lapse is a brief, non-significant return to a problem state, while a relapse is a more enduring, significant return to a problem state.

- [ ] View lapses in progress as part of the process of therapeutic change and as opportunities to use your rational thinking and constructive behavior, not as signs that you will inevitably relapse.

- [ ] Learn relapse prevention. This involves your identifying and dealing with situations in which you are likely to disturb yourself, rehearsing your rational beliefs while imagining facing these situations, and then rehearsing these beliefs in the situations themselves.

- [ ] You may disturb yourself about the prospect of a relapse. In this case, assume the worst. Assume that you will relapse and strive to think rationally about this. If you do this successfully, you will both undisturb yourself about this possibility and you will work steadily and unanxiously upon relapse prevention.

- ❑ Identify your vulnerabilities to self-disturbance and work steadily and sensibly on these issues in order to decrease your vulnerability.

- [ ] As you improve, decrease the frequency of therapy sessions so that you can take increasing responsibility for self-change.

- [ ] There are many different ways to terminate therapy. Discuss with your therapist these different ways and choose the way that is right for you.

- ❑ Ending therapy is not a once-and-for-all event. Just because you have finished therapy at a given point in time does not mean that you can't go back if you need to at a later date.

- [ ] Do not terminate self-therapy. If you do, you increase your likelihood that you will disturb yourself in the future.

- [ ] Use this book without becoming dependent on its use.

BOOKS, TAPES AND CDs

available from the Albert Ellis Institute

BASIC BOOKS ON REBT

- ☐ *Feeling Better, Getting Better, Staying Better,* Ellis, $15.95 (B203) 13 oz.
- ☐ *How to Stubbornly Refuse to Make Yourself Miserable About Anything — Yes, Anything!* Ellis, $12.95 (B009) 12 oz.
- ☐ *A Guide to Rational Living,* Ellis & Harper, $15.00 (B025) 9 oz.
- ☐ *How to Control Your Anxiety Before It Controls You,* Ellis, $19.95 (B190) 18 oz.
- ☐ *Overcoming Depression,* Hauck, $13.95 (B015) 6 oz.
- ☐ *Overcoming Procrastination,* Ellis & Knaus, $5.99 (B012) 5 oz.
- ☐ *Overcoming Destructive Beliefs, Feelings and Behaviors,* Ellis, $22.95 (B202) 24.5 oz.
- ☐ *Overcoming the Rating Game,* Hauck, $13.95 (B125) 6 oz.
- ☐ *Procrastination Workbook,* Knaus, $17.95 (B218) 18 oz.
- ☐ *Rational Counseling Primer,* Young, $2.50 (B061) 2.5 oz.
- ☐ *REBT Pocket Companion for Clients,* Dryden, $10.95 (B226) 7.8 oz.

Audiotapes

- ☐ *Action Jack Extracts the Core of REBT: An Interview with Albert Ellis,* $9.95 (C074) 2.5 oz.
- ☐ *Coming to Terms with Parents,* DiGiuseppe, $5.95 (C047) 2.5 oz.
- ☐ *Getting Over Getting Older,* Ellis, $9.95 (C073) 6 oz.
- ☐ *How to Control Your Anger Before It Controls You,* Ellis, $14.95 (C069) 6 oz.
- ☐ *How to Control Your Anxiety Before It Controls You,* Ellis, $14.95 (C072) 6 oz.
- ☐ *How to Stubbornly Refuse to be Ashamed of Anything,* Ellis, $9.95 (C010) 2.5 oz.
- ☐ *Learning to Relax,* Lazarus, $9.95 (C015) 2.5 oz.
- ☐ *Overcoming Procrastination,* Knaus, $9.95 (C018) 2.5 oz.
- ☐ *21 Ways to Stop Worrying,* Ellis, $9.95 (C026) 2.5 oz.

CD Rom

- ☐ *Managing Your Emotions,* DiMattia & Lega, $19.95 (CD001) 3.2 oz.

LOVE, SEX AND RELATIONSHIPS

- ☐ *Can Your Relationship Be Saved?* Broder, $15.95 (B208) 7.6 oz.
- ☐ *Guide to Successful Marriage,* Ellis & Harper, $7.00 (B006) 10.5 oz.
- ☐ *Head Over Heart in Love,* Borcherdt, $16.95 (B163) 9 oz.
- ☐ *How to Stop Destroying Your Relationships: A Guide to Enjoyable Dating, Mating and Relating,* Ellis & Harper, $21.95 (B204) 17.2 oz.
- ☐ *The Love Workbook: A Guide to Happiness in Your Personal Relationships,* Lima, $12.95 (B195) 16 oz.
- ☐ *Making Intimate Connections,* Ellis & Crawford, $15.95 (B199) 18 oz.
- ☐ *Men are from Earth, Women are from Earth,* Wenning, $18.95 (B192) 7 oz.
- ☐ *Overcoming Jealousy and Possessiveness,* Hauck, $13.95 (B004) 5 oz.
- ☐ *What to Do When* He *Has a Headache: Renewing Desire and Intimacy in Your Relationship,* Wolfe, $5.95 (B122) 7 oz.

Audiotapes

- ☐ *Conquering the Dire Need for Love,* Ellis, $5.95 (C003) 2.5 oz.
- ☐ *How to Achieve Healthy vs. Addictive Relationships,* Exner, $5.95 (C051) 2.5 oz.
- ☐ *How to Find a Love Relationship that Will Work for You,* Broder, $12.95 (C061) 2.5 oz.
- ☐ *Intelligent Person's Guide to Dating and Mating,* Ellis, $5.95 (C014) 2.5 oz.
- ☐ *Letting Go of Your Ended Love Relationship,* Broder, $8.95 (C053) 2.5 oz.
- ☐ *The Single Life: How to Make It Work for You,* Broder, $8.95 (C065) 2.5 oz.

ASSERTIVENESS AND ANGER MANAGEMENT

- ☐ *Anger: How to Live With and Without It (2nd ed.),* Ellis, $15.95 (B221) 12 oz.
- ☐ *How to Control Your Anger Before It Controls You,* Ellis & Tafrate, $12.95 (B180) 11 oz.
- ☐ *How to Live with a Neurotic,* Ellis, $7.00 (B005) 6.5 oz.
- ☐ *Managing and Understanding Parental Anger,* Barrish, $6.95 (B038) 4 oz.
- ☐ *Overcoming Frustration and Anger,* Hauck, $13.95 (B016) 5 oz.

Audiotapes

- ☐ *Conquering Low Frustration Tolerance,* Ellis, $9.95 (C004) 2.5 oz.
- ☐ *How to Control Your Anger Before It Controls You,* Ellis & Tafrate, $14.95 (C069) 6 oz.
- ☐ *What Do I Do with My Anger: Hold It In or Let It Out?,* DiGiuseppe, $9.95 (C012) 2.5 oz.
- ☐ *Self-Directed Sales Success,* DiMattia, $5.95 (C030) 2.5 oz.

HEALTHY LIVING

- ☐ *The Art and Science of Rational Eating,* Ellis & Abrams, $9.00 (B132) 25 oz.
- ☐ *How to Make Yourself Happy,* Ellis, $14.95 (B193) 12 oz.
- ☐ *Managing Addictions,* Bishop, $60.00 (B201) 30 oz.
- ☐ *Optimal Aging: Get Over Getting Older,* Ellis & Velten, $13.95 (B184) 15 oz.
- ☐ *Reason to Change: An REBT Workbook,* Dryden, $23.95 (B207) 22.9 oz.
- ☐ *Sex, Drugs, Gambling and Chocolate,* Horvath, $15.95 (B194) 20 oz.
- ☐ *When AA Doesn't Work for You: Rational Steps to Quitting Alcohol,* Ellis & Velten, $14.95 (B123) 18 oz.

HEALTHY LIVING *(cont'd)*

Audiotapes

- ☐ *Getting Over Getting Older,* Ellis, $9.95 (C073) 2.5 oz.
- ☐ *I'd Like to Stop, But… (Overcoming Addictions),* Ellis, $9.95 (C013) 2.5 oz.
- ☐ *Maximize the Moment: How to Have More Fun and Happiness in Life,* DiGiuseppe, $5.95 (C041) 2.5 oz.
- ☐ *Relapse Prevention Tape and Workbook,* Bishop, $22.95 (C050) 2.5 oz.

FOR PARENTS AND TEACHERS

- ☐ *Case Studies in REBT with Children and Adolescents,* Ellis & Wilde, $18.00 (B206) 9.1 oz.
- ☐ *Making Families Work and What to Do When They Don't,* Borcherdt, $15.95 (B165) 14 oz.
- ☐ *Managing and Understanding Parental Anger,* Barrish, $6.95 (B038) 4 oz.
- ☐ *Surviving and Enjoying Your Adolescent,* Barrish, $7.95 (B109) 6.5 oz.
- ☐ *Thinking, Feeling, Behaving: An Emotional Education Curriculum,* Vernon
  ____ Volume I (grades 1-6), $27.95 (B100) 27 oz.
  ____ Volume II (grades 7-12), $27.95 (B101) 27 oz.
- ☐ *Winning Cooperation from Your Child,* Wenning, $15.95 (B164) 6 oz.

Audiotapes

- ☐ *Coping with Parenting,* DiGiuseppe, $5.95 (C042) 2.5 oz.

FOR CHILDREN AND ADOLESCENTS

- ☐ *Homer the Homely Hound Dog,* Garcia /Pellegrini, $2.50 (B056) 5 oz.
- ☐ *Instant Replay,* Bedford, $1.95, (B073) 3 oz.
- ☐ *Rational Counseling Primer,* Young, $2.50 (B061) 2.5 oz.
- ☐ *Rational Stories for Children,* Waters, $4.00 (B044) 4.5 oz.
- ☐ *"Let's Get Rational" Game,* Wilde, $24.95 (SH026) 24 oz.

BOOKS FOR THERAPISTS

- ☐ *Overcoming Resistance (1st ed.),* Ellis, $25.00 (B065) 16.5 oz.
- ☐ *Overcoming Resistance (2nd ed.),* Ellis, $39.95 (B216) 19.8 oz.
- ☐ *The Practice of REBT,* Ellis & Dryden, $32.95 (B018S) 18 oz.
- ☐ *A Practitioner's Guide to REBT,* Walen, DiGiuseppe & Dryden, $34.95 (B001) 13 oz.
- ☐ *A Primer on REBT for Practitioners (2nd ed.),* Dryden, DiGiuseppe, & Neenan, $12.95 (B092) 6.1 oz.
- ☐ *Rational Emotive Behavior Group Therapy,* Dryden & Neenan, $30.95 (B213) 13.2 oz.
- ☐ *Rational Emotive Behavior Therapy: A Therapist's Guide,* Ellis & MacLaren, $21.95 (B189) 16 oz.
- ☐ *Reaching Their Minds: A Trainer's Manual,* DiMattia & Ijzermans, $10.95 (B159) 6 oz.
- ☐ *Reason and Emotion in Psychotherapy,* Ellis, $22.95 (B014) 32 oz.
- ☐ *REBT Resource Book for Practitioners (2nd ed.),* Bernard & Wolfe, Eds., $49.95 (B196) 3 lbs.
- ☐ *REBT Therapist's Pocket Companion,* Dryden & Neenan, $10.95 (B225) 7.8 oz.
- ☐ *RET with Alcoholics and Substance Abusers,* Ellis et al., $31.50 (B023) 9 oz.
- ☐ *Special Applications of REBT,* Dryden & Yankura, $32.95 (B179) 10 oz.
- ☐ *Teoría y Práctica de la Terapia Racional Emotivo-Conductual,* Lega, Caballo & Ellis, $10.95 (B209) 6.8 oz.
- ☐ *What Works When with Children & Adolescents,* Vernon, $39.95 (B215) 34 oz.